THE KOREAN WAR

"The Forgotten War"

R. Conrad Stein

—American War Series—

Enslow Publishers, Inc.

40 Industrial Road	PO Box 38
Box 398	Aldershot
Berkeley Heights, NJ 07922	Hants GU12 6BP
USA	UK

http://www.enslow.com

> ...se the United States had not gone on a true war footing ...cause only a relatively small number of men were involved, ...pared to the huge national effort in World War II, Korea soon became known as the Forgotten War."
>
> —Bevin Alexander, as quoted from his book, *KOREA: The First War We Lost,* by Hippocrene Books, New York.

Library of Congress Cataloging-in-Publication Data

Stein, R. Conrad.
    The Korean War : "The forgotten war" / R. Conrad Stein.
       p. cm. — (American war series)
    Includes bibliographical references and index.
    ISBN 0-7660-1729-X (pbk)
    ISBN 0-89490-526-0 (library ed.)
    1. Korean War, 1950-1953—Juvenile literature. 2. Korean War, 1950-1953—United States—Juvenile literature. [1. Korean War, 1950-1953.] I. Title. II. Series.
    DS918.S75 1994
    951.904'2—dc20   94-565
                                  CIP
                                  AC

Printed in the United States of America

10 9 8 7 6

To Our Readers: All Internet addresses in this book were active and appropriate when we went to press. Any comments or suggestions can be sent by e-mail to Comments@enslow.com or to the address on the back cover.

Illustration Credits: Courtesy of the Prints and Photographs Division, Library of Congress, pp. 13, 15, 31, 33, 35, 51, 61, 70, 77, 81, 88, 90, 103, 105; Enslow Publishers, Inc., pp. 11, 111; National Air and Space Museum, Smithsonian Institution, pp. 95, 97; Courtesy of the National Archives, pp. 7, 19, 21, 24, 27, 29, 38, 40, 42, 44, 47, 53, 55, 57, 63, 65, 72, 74, 83, 85, 93, 101, 107.

Cover Illustration: Courtesy of the National Archives.

Contents

Foreword

In 1953 the fighting in Korea ended, and a Marine from Chicago finally came home. The Marine was old enough to remember the conclusion of World War II, at which time returning veterans triumphantly marched through the heart of downtown. Thousands of people lined the streets during that parade and cheered the heroes. When the Chicago Marine returned from Korea, a neighbor asked him, "Hey, I haven't seen you for a while. Have you been out of town?"

The Korean War is called "the Forgotten War." It was largely ignored while it was being fought. And today it is a footnote rather than a chapter in many history books.

From its beginnings, the Korean War was misunderstood at home. It had no terrible trigger similar to the Japanese sneak attack on Pearl Harbor, which infuriated Americans and sent them storming into World War II. Unlike World War II, defeating the enemy in Korea did not seem vital to the American way of life. It became a hated war, but Americans thought there was little they could do to bring it to an end. As the Korean conflict stretched into its second and third years, the public simply lost interest in it.

Yet some 54,000 Americans died in Korea during the war years. Deaths at the front shattered families at home, giving them the same wrenching grief familiar to all wars. Though it is called "the Forgotten War," it is remembered by the millions who suffered in the conflict. And for the families who lost loved ones, the Korean War will never be forgotten.

"Mr. President, I have very serious news. The North Koreans have invaded South Korea."

— A telephone call from Secretary of State Dean Acheson to President Harry S. Truman.

1 Thunder Before the Storm

 Sunday—3:30 A.M. (Korean time)—June 25, 1950. U.S. Army Captain Joseph Darrigo jumped out of bed. An earthshaking explosion had jarred him awake. Another powerful explosion caused the floor of his hut to tremble. What was going on? Why was the South Korean Army firing artillery at this time of morning? Suddenly a thought electrified Darrigo. These shell bursts did not come from South Korean guns because they were hitting too close. The furious blasts could mean only one thing: the North Korean army was shelling South Korea.

Darrigo ran outside to his jeep. The sky was black, and along the northern horizon he saw muzzle flashes from what seemed to be a thousand cannons. He started the jeep and sped north. Darrigo was the only American in the vicinity of the 38th Parallel, the artificial boundary that separated North Korea from South Korea. For six months he had served in the region as an American adviser to the South Korean army. He had seen many instances of sniping and artillery exchanges between army units of the two Koreas. The Americans called the skirmishes between north and south "rice wars." But this artillery bombardment was too intense to be another rice war. No, this time something important was taking place—something terrible.

Speeding down the twisting mountain roads, Darrigo approached the city of Kaesong. Shells whined and crashed ever closer. Still he felt a burning need to find out what was happening. Several major roads intersected in Kaesong, making it a prime target for any army wanting to invade the south.

The shelling had lifted, and the first rays of sun streaked the sky as Darrigo reached the outskirts of town. He braked his jeep to a screaming halt. Ahead was a train stopped on its tracks. Hundreds of North Korean soldiers swarmed off the train while their officers barked out commands. Now there were no lingering doubts. The North Koreans had invaded South Korea.

Shots rang out, and bullets thudded into the earth near Darrigo's jeep. The North Koreans had spotted him. The captain jammed his jeep into reverse, screeching it backward. Quickly he spun the jeep around and

President Harry Truman ordered American troops to Korea in late June, 1950.

raced out of Kaesong, leaving the invading troops behind. He was the lone American witness to a surprise attack that would no doubt plunge his nation into war. Darrigo's duty was to tell his superiors of the surprise attack.[1]

But Army headquarters had already received word of artillery fire along the 38th Parallel. Emergency radio dispatches were sent to General Douglas MacArthur in Tokyo and to President Harry Truman's office in Washington, D.C. In the nation's capitol the news struck like a dark note of thunder. Once more America had fallen into the grips of war.

"[I experienced] an uncanny feeling of nightmare. . . . The same fell note of war cry was again ringing in my ears. It couldn't be, I told myself. Not again! Not again!"

—General Douglas MacArthur, remembering his thoughts when he was told North Korea had attacked South Korea, thereby igniting war.

2 War Comes to a Troubled Land

 Korea is a peninsula that juts out of the Asian landmass like a fat thumb. It is roughly the shape of Florida, but about 30 percent larger than that American state. It is a mountainous land where rivers run swiftly and cut deep gouges into the earth. Trees in Korea are little more than bushes, and few flowers push out of the country's rocky soil. Rarely does one hear a bird sing in Korea.

Historic Korea

This land, which many Americans considered to be uninviting and even hostile, had long been a breeding ground for war. A glance at a map shows that the Korean peninsula is a virtual land bridge between China and

Japan. For centuries each of the two Asian giants looked upon Korea as their enemies' avenue leading to the homeland. An old Japanese saying claimed, "Korea is a dagger pointed at our hearts," while the Chinese said the peninsula is "a hammer pointed at our heads." In the late 1800s, Russia expanded to touch Korea's borders, and the luckless country became a pawn fought over by three aggressive states.

In 1910 Imperial Japan formally annexed Korea, making it a colony. Koreans had endured many masters, but none more harsh than the Japanese. The Imperial government stripped land from the peasants and gave it to Japanese nationals. Koreans who protested were beaten, jailed, or executed by beheading. Despite the brutal punishments, Koreans rallied behind leaders who promised to liberate the nation from Japanese rule.

One independence leader was Syngman Rhee, the son of a Korean scholar. Because of his pro-independence stand, Rhee was jailed, tortured, and forced to flee Korea. He escaped to the United States, where he lived in exile for twenty years.

Kim Il Sung was another Korean nationalist who commanded a large following. He joined Korean exiles in China and looked to the Communist Party to deliver independence to his country. While in China he studied guerrilla warfare and fought with the Chinese communists against the Japanese.

On August 15, 1945, Japan surrendered to the Allied nations, ending World War II. Now Syngman Rhee,

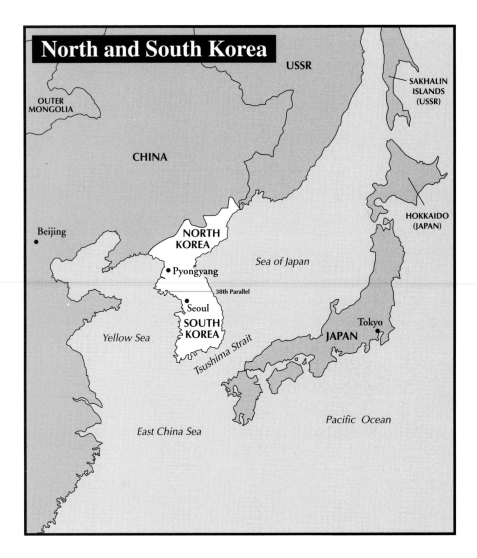

North and South Korea

USSR

SAKHALIN
ISLANDS
(USSR)

OUTER
MONGOLIA

CHINA

HOKKAIDO
(JAPAN)

Beijing

NORTH
KOREA

Sea of Japan

Pyongyang

38th Parallel

Seoul

SOUTH
KOREA

Yellow Sea

Tsushima Strait

Tokyo

JAPAN

East China Sea

Pacific Ocean

Kim Il Sung, and millions of other Koreans looked forward to freedom and independence for Korea.

A Shrimp Crushed in a Battle of Whales

An old Korean proverb goes: "A shrimp is crushed in a battle between whales." The saying refers to Korean history and the sad fact that the tiny nation has so often been a casualty in wars between its more powerful neighbors. To Korea's misfortune, the post-World War II years proved to be a repeat of that dismal history.

Days before the Japanese surrender, the Russians entered the war and poured thousands of troops into Japanese-occupied Manchuria. Russian soldiers quickly advanced as far as the northern reaches of Korea. American leaders feared the entire peninsula would fall under Russian control. Hoping to stem the Russian advance, a group of United States Army officers and diplomats arranged an emergency meeting in Washington, D.C. There they studied a map of Korea that they borrowed from a local college. One of the group's members was U.S. Army Colonel Dean Rusk, who later served as Secretary of State under President John F. Kennedy.

Rusk and the others proposed drawing a line across the middle of Korea at the 38th Parallel. North of the line would be a Russian sphere of influence, south of the line an American sphere of influence. The Americans sent their plan to Moscow, and to everyone's surprise, the Russians accepted the proposal without argument. Dean Rusk later admitted the entire meeting, which determined the fate of Korea for decades to

Korean farmers plant rice in paddies. Korea's mountainous terrain and rocky soil make it difficult to grow food.

come, took the Americans only thirty minutes to conclude.

The 38th Parallel was an arbitrary boundary, created entirely for the convenience of the superpowers. The hastily drawn line divided a unified people. There was no difference between a South Korean and a North Korean in terms of culture—not even language. At first, both the Russians and the Americans believed the division of Korea would be temporary. Both sides presumed elections would soon take place, allowing a single government to take charge of the entire land. But before elections could be held, the Cold War—a period of tension between communist and non-communist nations—began. Because of Cold War pressures, the Russians refused to allow international election commissioners to come north of the 38th Parallel, while the Americans in the south resisted any political party that even hinted at communism.

Instead of one independent country, two staunchly opposite states emerged in Korea. In the north, the Russians organized the Democratic People's Republic. In the south the Republic of Korea rose. South Korea was led by Syngman Rhee, who was almost seventy years old when he took power. Rhee claimed to be pro-democracy, but he jailed and even murdered his political opponents. The North Korean chief was Kim Il Sung, a dedicated communist. Each leader claimed he was the true voice of all Korea. The two men hated and vowed to overthrow one another.

Complicating the situation in the two Koreas was a

South Korean President Syngman Rhee poses here with General Van Fleet. Because of his pro-independence beliefs, Rhee was forced to live in exile in the United States for twenty years.

civil war that began years earlier in China and heated up during World War II. The civil war pitted the Chinese republican government against a strong force of Chinese communists. In 1949 the communist forces won the civil war, and the remnants of the Nationalist government were forced to flee to the nearby island of Taiwan. Now the communist Chinese, loosely allied with the Russians, stood on North Korea's border. The Korean peninsula became what diplomats called a "hot spot."

To this day it is not clear what influence the Russians or the Chinese communists had over North Korea's decision to launch its sudden invasion. Certainly Joseph Stalin, the Russian premier, was aware of Kim Il Sung's plan to attack South Korea. Stalin looked upon Korea in Cold War terms. He hoped the conflict would extend communism without directly involving Russian troops. The Korean people, who were doomed to enormous suffering, became a chess piece in the Cold War. Once more in its history, Korea was "a shrimp crushed in a battle between whales."

A Police Action

At the time of the North Korean attack, the United Nations (UN) was a five-year-old institution. It was born in the waning days of World War II, when people believed the post-war world would be one of peace and prosperity. The organization offered its member states collective security. In theory all the nations of the UN would act to defeat an aggressor that broke the peace by assaulting its neighbor.

However, from its infancy, the UN's effectiveness was hampered by the Cold War. When North Korea invaded, Russia was boycotting UN meetings because the world body had refused to allow communist China to have the permanent seat reserved for it on the Security Council. Ironically, the Russian boycott strengthened America's hand in the UN. In an emergency meeting called on June 25, 1950, the UN Security Council demanded that North Korea cease fire and withdraw to its border. Had the Russians been present at the meeting, they surely would have vetoed the council's declaration.

The next move in the drama unfolding in Korea belonged to American President Harry S. Truman. The president was delighted with the strongly worded declaration that emerged from the UN. The declaration gave him UN authority to send American troops to Korea if the North Koreans refused to withdraw. Reports from the front indicated that the North Koreans were marching aggressively southward, showing no sign of pulling back to the 38th Parallel. Therefore Truman ordered the United States military to go to Korea and stop the aggressors. The president told a news conference, "The members of the United Nations are going to the relief of the Korean republic, to suppress a bandit raid."

By sending troops to Korea the president committed his country to a limited war, one designed to stop an aggressor rather than defeat an entire nation. The American public was not accustomed to fighting wars on a limited scale. From the start Korea was a different, and a confusing undertaking. At first, the president refused to use the word "war" in connection with Korea. Finally one reporter asked if the Korean intervention was "a police action under the UN?" Truman answered, "Yes, that is exactly what it amounts to." So, the Korean War was a police action.

The North Korean Surge

On the fighting front disaster loomed. Relentlessly the North Koreans drove into the heart of the south. The North Korean army was a well-trained, splendidly equipped fighting force. Many of their officers and their senior enlisted men had served in the Russian or the communist Chinese infantry during World War II. They were combat-hardened and accustomed to victory. Spearheading the North Korean advance were Russian-built T-34 tanks—the same steel giants that stopped the Germans at Stalingrad in World War II. Weighing thirty tons and armed with a high-velocity 85mm gun, the T-34s rolled steadily over the roads and rice paddies south of the 38th Parallel. No rival tank in Asia could outfight this Russian warhorse.

The harried South Koreans prepared a defensive line along the Han River that flowed through Seoul, the South Korean capital. In desperation South Korean engineers blew up bridges on the Han, even though 10,000 of their own troops were left stranded on the northern side of the river. One bridge at Seoul was exploded despite the fact that it was crammed with civilians, army troops, and vehicles. At least 500 people perished as the bridge toppled into the river.

The Russian-built T-34 was one of World War II's best tanks. The North Korean version of the T-34 was similar to the one pictured here except it had North Korean markings.

Panic seized the city of Seoul. Government officials, including President Syngman Rhee, fled the capital as the North Korean army approached the city limits. Families of American Embassy staff were packed into trucks and hurried to the port of Inchon for evacuation by sea.

On the fifth day of the war, General Douglas Mac-Arthur took off on a transport plane from Tokyo and landed at a frontline airfield. MacArthur was a World War II hero, and the choice of many Americans to be president of the United States. Even though he was seventy years old, he looked trim and athletic. As his transport plane approached the field, a North Korean fighter swooped down upon it. Everyone on board recoiled in fear, but MacArthur calmly looked out the window as an American P-51 chased the intruder away. Unflinching courage under fire was MacArthur's signature.

After climbing out of the plane, MacArthur and his staff boarded jeeps and drove toward the front lines. A depressing scene greeted them. Streams of retreating South Korean troops and exhausted civilians wound over the roads, marching slowly southward. The civilians especially wore the pathetic looks of a defeated nation. Dazed, many of them wounded, they seemed to be wandering with little purpose. Great mosses of these civilians remained wandering refugees for years to come.

On a hill overlooking the Han River the motorcade stopped, and MacArthur stepped out of the jeep. Shell fire rocked the earth near him. In the distance huge

South Korean children, made homeless by the war, search for scraps of food in the rubble of a railroad yard near Seoul.

columns of smoke rose from scores of fires raging in Seoul. The general stood observing the battlefront for more than half an hour. Finally he simply said, "Let's go." MacArthur later wrote in his memoirs that he spent his brief time on the hilltop planning a counterattack, which included a massive landing at nearby Inchon.

Meanwhile, the North Korean offensive steamrolled forward. Seoul fell to the North Koreans in less than a week. After just ten days of fighting, 44,000 South Korean troops—almost half the country's total force—were reported killed, captured, or missing.

"Where's Korea?"

To American soldiers in 1950, Japan was known as "easy duty." A lowly American PFC stationed in occupied Japan earned more than a Japanese schoolteacher. In the barracks, soldiers were waited on by laundry and shoeshine boys. Many men supported girlfriends in the villages. It is no wonder the troops grumbled when they were ordered to pack their gear and board planes for Korea. Korea! Where's that?

The first group to arrive was a hastily assembled contingent of 400 infantrymen called Task Force Smith. Commanded by Lieutenant Colonel Charles B. Smith, the men landed at an airfield near the port city of Pusan. There they climbed aboard boxcars to take a long train ride to the fighting front. One member of the task force was First Lieutenant William Wyrick. "During our trip north I saw wounded South Koreans coming back from the fighting," Wyrick wrote. "On the next track was one car after another loaded with wounded. It was a very heartrending sight."[1]

Task Force Smith was ordered to dig in and hold defensive positions until stronger American units could arrive. Despite the many dead and wounded South Koreans they had seen, the soldiers were confident they could beat back the North Koreans. They believed enemy troops would panic and run as soon as they realized they were fighting American infantrymen. Many of the men told each other they would be back in their comfortable barracks in Japan in just a few days.

A soaking rain drenched the Americans on July 5, 1950, as they dug foxholes on a hill near the city of Taejon. The constant showers put them in a dismal mood. They cursed Korea and the enemy that had brought them to this foul land. Then, peering through binoculars into the sweeping rain, an officer spotted tanks. The huge machines rumbled over a road that twisted through rice paddies. A chilling fear swept over the Americans. They had expected to see a few enemy tanks, but now in the distance they counted thirty or more. Behind the tanks came waves of foot soldiers, crouching as they walked, each one carrying a light machine gun.

American 105mm cannons opened fire, and shells exploded among the tanks. The North Korean crews buttoned up—closed the hatches on their machines—and kept churning forward. Task Force Smith's soldiers trembled in their foxholes. Most were young and had never before suffered through combat.

Officers and sergeants screamed at the men to fire

Grief-stricken American soldiers mourn over the loss of a buddy killed on the Korean front in August of 1950.

their rifles and machine guns. Instead the Americans gazed at the advancing tanks with an eerie sense of detachment, as if they were watching this amazing scene on a newsreel.

Finally bazooka teams crept close to the lead T-34. The bazookas (rocket launchers) were designed early in World War II and shot a 2.36-inch shell. A gunner fired a rocket at the lead tank, but to everyone's horror the bazooka shell failed to penetrate the thick-skinned enemy machine. Again and again the Americans fired. One team shot twenty-two rockets at one tank, but the T-34 plodded ahead like a giant unaware of the stings of a mosquito. A lieutenant named Charles Payne said, "Hitting the T-34 head-on merely produced a bounce-off. We soon ran out of ammo and had one man killed in action. I pulled everyone back."[2]

Commander Smith tried to lead his men on an orderly retreat from the hilltop position, but North Korean tanks had advanced too close. Fearing they would be crushed under tank treads, men bolted from their foxholes and scrambled downhill. Many left their rifles on the ground. Dead and wounded men were abandoned at the battlefront. Task Force Smith—the unit that arrived in Korea brimming with confidence—was routed.

*"He was covered with worms. He was just
laying there, all covered with worms. Oh Jesus,
the worms were—"*
  —A newspaper writer describing a young American soldier
  who had been brought into a field hospital.

3   The UN Offensive

 It was brutally hot and humid on July 13, 1950, when the 24th Infantry Division reached the southern banks of the Kum River. Days earlier the soldiers of the 24th had been shipped to Korea from bases in Japan. Sweat drenched the men's clothes as they dug foxholes. Rice paddies in checkerboard patterns covered practically every foot of level ground in South Korea. The tiny rice fields were fertilized with human waste. No Korean War veteran ever forgot the pungent smell that hung in the air over the rice country, especially on rainy days. Sarcastically the men asked each other why they were preparing to defend a land that smelled so awful. So far the members of the 24th

Men of the 24th Infantry Division were among the first to arrive in Korea. Here they move up to the frontlines in July 1950.

Division had not heard of the disaster that struck Task Force Smith.

"Fall Back!"

Darkness fell, and a terrible night began. Explosions shook the earth as mighty Russian-made 122mm guns raked the riverbank. Even the World War II veterans who had suffered through German shelling were shocked by the fury of the bombardment. Then, looking into moonlight, the Americans saw enemy troops swimming and pushing rafts toward them from across the river. Parachute flares fired from American artillery pieces turned night into blazing day. Machine guns cut down the advancing North Koreans. Still the enemy pressed forward, sometimes stepping on the backs of fallen comrades. In shallow spots, North Korean tanks splashed across the Kum River. Unable to stop the tanks, American units pulled back. When one sector collapsed, another was forced to follow suit or risk being surrounded. Soon the entire 24th Division was in general retreat.

South of the Kum River, the city of Taejon fell to the North Koreans on July 20. General William Dean, the commander of the 24th Infantry Division, raced among his men urging them to stand and fight. Dean personally led bazooka teams on tank-hunting missions to destroy the North Korean T-34s. But not even the general's heroism could stop the flight. Dean and a handful of soldiers found themselves stranded in Taejon while the rest of the division fled southward. The general

An American machine gun crew in action along the Korean front.

roamed the hills near the city for a month before he was captured and became the highest-ranking prisoner of war (POW) in the Korean conflict. He was later awarded the Congressional Medal of Honor for his heroism at Taejon.

During July, the words "fall back!" echoed over the Korean front. Army public relations officers called the withdrawals a "fighting retreat." But the men knew they were being overpowered by a determined foe. A grim joke ran through the American ranks. Question: What's the difference between a North Korean and a South Korean? Answer: He's a South Korean if he's running *with* you; he's a North Korean if he's running *after* you.

Experts still argue why United States forces were so ineffective in the early stages of the Korean War. Many observers believe the Americans were spoiled by the soft life they enjoyed in occupied Japan and Okinawa. Easy living does not make for tough soldiers. Also, Army ranks were weakened by the quick demobilization that took place after World War II. Most divisions were operating at only 70 percent of their wartime manpower. Army planners in those days believed the next war would be fought by airplanes dropping atomic bombs, so they allowed the combat efficiency of conventional units to erode. No one expected to fight a war like the one in Korea—a scaled-down, but bloody, version of World War II.

The South Korean army, too, was unable to stop the hard-driving North Koreans. South Korea lacked the tanks and long-range guns that the North Koreans were

Major General William F. Dean, the highest-ranking American POW of the war, plays a game with one of his captors in a POW camp in North Korea. This photo was taken while Dean awaited release.

now using with brutal effectiveness. The United States had been reluctant to give the South Koreans offensive weapons such as tanks because American leaders feared Syngman Rhee would make an unwarranted attack on the north. On the other hand, the Russians had no such qualms and equipped the North Koreans with ample tanks and artillery pieces.

The Pusan Perimeter

General Walton Walker, the overall ground commander in Korea, was desperate. "There will be no more retreating," he told his officers in what later was remembered as the most stirring battlefront speech of the Korean War. "There is no line behind us to which we can retreat. . . . We must fight until the end. . . . I want everybody to understand that we are going to hold this line. We are going to win."[1]

Walker made his famous speech on July 29, 1950. At the time, United States forces and the remnants of the South Korean army had dug in along a horseshoe-shaped 145-mile front called the Pusan Perimeter. Behind the men lay the ocean; ahead stood the enemy. Walker was determined to fight to the death for this last remaining toehold on the Korean peninsula.

Sensing final victory, the North Koreans threw terrifying human-wave charges against the Pusan defenders. "GI die! GI die!" the North Koreans shouted as they raced recklessly into American positions. An Army PFC named Robert Harper remembered, "At times the fighting [on the Pusan Perimeter] got so bad we would have

United States Marines surround a wounded North Korean soldier.

to pull off the line and let the enemy have a hill or ridge. . . . Next day we would counterattack and drive the North Koreans back. That's the way it went: seesaw, back and forth."[2]

For six agonizing weeks the Pusan Perimeter held, despite the fury of enemy attacks. By fending off the communists, the men on the front bought precious time for a great buildup of troops taking place further to the rear. The 1st Cavalry Division arrived from Japan and the 2nd Infantry Division was shipped all the way from bases in the United States. In early August, the 1st Marine Brigade—a spirited, combat-ready outfit—climbed off ships at Pusan Harbor. Troops from other UN countries—Great Britain, France, and the Netherlands—began to arrive. Pershing M-26 tanks, mounting 90mm guns, entered the battle. The huge American-built machines were more than a match for the T-34s. Infantrymen defending the Pusan front received 3.5-inch rocket launchers, a big brother of the World War II bazooka. The new tanks and rocket launchers gradually reduced the North Korean tank advantage.

Also, the constant battering at the Pusan front began to sap the strength of the North Korean army. Thousands of the enemy's best troops were killed or wounded. The casualties were replaced by poorly trained teenaged soldiers who were recruited at the point of a bayonet. Also, the North Korean supply lines now stretched 200 miles or more to their home bases. Truck convoys and supply trains were relentlessly bombed and strafed by American fighter planes taking off from airfields in

American troops at the port of Pusan fought off the North Koreans during six weeks of brutal combat.

Japan. The American aircraft swept enemy planes from the sky and roamed freely over the Pusan Perimeter.

Slowly the bloody Pusan defense began to transform American soldiers from soft garrison troops into hardened fighting units. In many ways, the ordeal at Pusan was similar to the terrible winter General George Washington faced at Valley Forge. Washington's men suffered near collapse in the winter of 1777–1778, but emerged from Valley Forge as a toughened new army. The same grim conversion took place at Pusan, but at a terrible price in blood. In six weeks of vicious combat, almost 20,000 Americans were killed or wounded. An infantry lieutenant named Bart DeLashmet commented, "You had to feel sorry for our troops. Most of them were kids who hadn't learned how to soldier. They had to learn that in the Pusan Perimeter, and they had to learn the hard way."[3]

End Run at Inchon

In Japan, General MacArthur made bold plans to break the deadlock at Pusan. From the time he first saw the enemy pouring into the south near Seoul, he had envisioned a grand counterattack that would come from the sea. Inchon, the port that served Seoul, was the focus of his thoughts. A landing by U.S. Marines at Inchon would enable the Americans to capture Seoul and cut off supplies for the North Korean army. It would also take the enemy by surprise. In football terms, an Inchon assault would be the equivalent of an end run around the opposition's line.

The Navy, however, insisted a landing at Inchon was impossible. General Lemuel Shepherd, the fleet Marine commander, agreed. Tides at Inchon were among the trickiest in the world. There was no beach on the mainland. Assault boats would have to edge up to a high sea wall and Marines in the boats would be forced to climb ladders to reach the shore. All this would take place under enemy artillery and machine gun fire. The Inchon landing was a terrible idea, said Navy and Marine officers, a disaster in the making.

At an August 23 conference, General MacArthur listened to the objections. After waiting for his turn to speak, he pointed out the advantages to an Inchon invasion. First, since the landings seemed to be a physical impossibility, the North Korean command would place only light defenses at Inchon. Second, Inchon was 180 miles north of the Pusan Perimeter, and only a short distance from Seoul. A recapture of Seoul would put a dagger in the backs of the North Koreans at the Pusan front. The communists would be caught in the jaws of a powerful vice. MacArthur called Pusan a "bloody perimeter," where Americans were being killed "like beef cattle in a slaughterhouse." The general ended his speech at the conference on a dramatic note: "I can almost hear the ticking of the second hand of destiny. . . . We shall land at Inchon, and I shall crush them."[4] End of discussion: the commander had spoken.

On September 15, a mighty armada of 261 ships approached the waters off Inchon. With deafening roars, Navy gunboats opened fire on shore defenses. Heaviest

The huge battleship U.S.S. *Missouri* pounds shore targets deep in Korea.

of all the warships was the newly recommissioned U.S.S. *Missouri*, on whose decks the Japanese government officially surrendered five years earlier. Now the mighty *Missouri* pounded communist strong points with its 16-inch guns. Planes from four aircraft carriers buzzed overhead, dropping bombs and peppering the landing areas with their machine guns. A correspondent on one of the ships said the shore "looked like a giant forest fire."

More than 70,000 soldiers and Marines waited in transports to storm the shoreline. First the Marines had to take a large offshore island called Wolmi-Do. At 7:00 A.M. a Marine battalion riding tiny assault craft hit Wolmi-Do's rocky beach. The Marines captured the island in forty-five minutes at a cost of only seventeen men wounded. General MacArthur, who watched the operation from the command ship U.S.S. *Mt. McKinley*, was overjoyed at the early success. After the island's conquest he was confident he had achieved the all-important element of surprise.

In the late afternoon a wave of assault boats churned toward Inchon to begin the main landings. This was the most perilous part of the invasion scheme. The boats had only two hours to race into Inchon Harbor, discharge the Marines, and roar back to sea. Tides at Inchon varied thirty-five feet. The invasion had to take place during the precious hours of high tide. At low tide the entire harbor became a shallow swamp. Boats caught in this muck would be easy targets for North Korean gunners.

At 5:30 P.M., the first group of Navy assault craft

General Douglas MacArthur, center, observes the naval bombardment of Inchon from the deck of his command ship, the U.S.S. *Mt. McKinley* on September 15, 1950.

bumped up against the Inchon seawall. So far the scheduling was perfect, and the boats had ample time to return to sea and escape being trapped by low tides. In the boats, Marines slammed ladders against the seawall, and scrambled up as scattered enemy fire poured over them. In a bizarre way the men looked like soldiers of times long past, who scaled the walls of medieval castles.

By nightfall the Marines had swept over Inchon and were digging in on the outskirts of the city to fend off possible counterattacks. Resistance was surprisingly light. Truly the communists had been hit where they least expected a blow. MacArthur gambled at Inchon—and he won.

On September 17, the Americans overran Kimpo Airfield near Inchon. The airstrip was ideally located and vital for both sides. Just hours after its capture, planes were landing and taking off from the battered field. With Kimpo Airfield secure, American forces turned toward their ultimate objective—Seoul.

A Marine PFC named John Bishop first saw the South Korean capital from a hill outside of town. "I'll never forget the sight," Bishop said,

> Down below was a big city . . . smoke was coming from everywhere. Buildings and houses were on fire. You could see Corsairs [Marine and Navy piston-driven fighter planes] dive down from the sky, then swoop back up, leaving behind a puff of black smoke and a dull explosion. From the top of the hill it looked like I was watching a movie. Except it was for real.[5]

Marines use ladders to storm the shores of Inchon.

The fight for Seoul was a desperate struggle—street by street and house by house. Casualties on both sides were staggering as the battle dragged on for three days. Civilians suffered the most casualties. Unarmed and terrified, the capital's women, children, and elderly huddled in flimsy houses while bombs and shells obliterated entire neighborhoods. A young Marine named Francis Killeen, while fighting in a Seoul neighborhood, saw a crowd of wounded and frightened civilians and said, "It was a sorry sight. One Korean civilian—he seemed to be the leader of a neighborhood—stood crying uncontrollably, holding a wounded little girl in his arms. He handed her to [our medic], who took the little one from him, laid her on the ground, and covered her with a poncho."[6]

On September 28, General MacArthur and South Korean president Syngman Rhee drove triumphantly into Seoul, riding in a shiny black limousine. The city was in ruins, and dense clouds of smoke poured from hundreds of fires as the limousine approached the national capitol building. Outside the building, while bands played and children waved South Korean flags, Rhee made a patriotic speech. At its conclusion he turned to MacArthur, grasped the general's hand, and said, "We love you as the savior of our race."

Home by Christmas

The Inchon landing was planned to coincide with a massive breakout at the Pusan Perimeter. At first, blinding sheets of rain turned roads near Pusan into mire, and

Deadly combat took place on the streets of Seoul, South Korea, as UN troops fought their way into the city in September 1950.

stymied an advance. But when the skies cleared, American planes struck viciously at enemy defenses. Napalm—one of the most horrible weapons in the arsenal of conventional warfare—was used with devastating effects. Napalm bombs are huge canisters filled with jellied gasoline. Upon striking the ground the canister breaks open, spreading flaming fluid over a wide area—searing everything it touches.

Massive air attacks helped break the enemy's will to fight along the Pusan Perimeter. North Korean officers who knew of the Inchon operation, feared their supply lines had been severed. The North Korean troops were deliberately kept in the dark about the successful landing to their rear. By the last week in September, UN forces had broken out of the Pusan front and were tearing northward. American morale was high. "We knew we had them on the run," said one soldier. "We wanted to just keep going because we were all thinking the war would be over and we could go home." On September 28, American forces racing out of Pusan linked up with the Inchon front. Almost all of South Korea was now in UN hands.

The drama of the war shifted back to Washington, D.C., and to UN headquarters at Lake Success, New York. A debate raged: Should the UN armies cross the 38th Parallel and conquer North Korea? Many diplomats worried that the Russians would intervene in the war to prevent the defeat of their North Korean allies. An even greater menace were the Chinese communists who occupied Manchuria, just to the north of the

Korean peninsula. The diplomats asked each other if Red China would cross the Yalu River—the border that separates Manchuria from North Korea—and turn what started as a limited war into a larger and even bloodier conflict.

General MacArthur assured diplomats in Washington and in the UN that neither the Chinese nor the Russians would enter Korea. The general claimed his "sources" informed him North Korea stood on its own in this conflict. He urged President Truman to let him cross the 38th Parallel and destroy the remnants of the North Korean army. Truman agreed. On October 7, the UN General Assembly also authorized MacArthur to enter North Korea and establish "a unified, independent, and democratic government" throughout Korea.

Now commanding a powerful army, MacArthur stormed into North Korea in early October 1950. His forces consisted of seven American divisions, a like number of South Korean troops, and units from Great Britain, France, Turkey, the Netherlands, Australia, and the Philippines. American bombers and fighter planes ranged freely over the length and width of Korea. Warships shelled targets at will on either side of the peninsula. The general sensed a quick victory.

While advancing north, UN troops found the rugged terrain to be a greater obstacle than the enemy. North Korea is even more mountainous than the south. The roads were primitive or nonexistent. Trucks were unable to twist through the narrow mountain passes, resulting in heavy artillery pieces being left behind.

Navy fighter bombers (World War II era F4U Corsairs) circle the aircraft carrier U.S.S. *Boxer* in Korean waters.

MacArthur divided his forces to cover the terrain faster. Military historians later severely criticized the general for splitting his troops. The enemy—many of them still full of fight—hid in mountain crags and ambushed UN troops on the march. Still the UN offensive continued. "Day and night we kept going," said a weary infantryman. "We slept in full combat gear. There was little time for eating. Hot chow never caught up to us."

Pyongyang, the North Korean capital, fell to the UN on October 19. Then on October 26, an American patrol captured an enemy soldier dressed in a strange uniform. After questioning the soldier, an officer discovered he was Chinese. Four days later, sixteen more Chinese troops were captured deep in North Korea.

Once more MacArthur told the world there was no danger of a massive Chinese intervention in the war. The general claimed the Chinese troops picked up in North Korea were just a few communist zealots who crossed the Yalu River under their own volition. Nothing would quell MacArthur's confidence. He even hinted to news reporters that he would have the boys "home by Christmas."

Most Americans trusted MacArthur. In World War II he was a leading architect of "island hopping," a grand strategy that brought American forces toward the Japanese heartland. The surprise invasion of Inchon proved the seventy-year-old general was still a tactical genius. Let MacArthur win this war any way he wishes, thought the American public. With "Mac" in charge, nothing can go wrong.

"We didn't know what the hell was going on until they [the Chinese] came at us. That was when we fought for our lives."
—A U.S. Marine at the Chosin Reservoir.

4 A New War

Despite the presence of a few Chinese troops, final victory in the Korean War seemed to be near. In late October 1950, a South Korean regiment reached the Yalu River. Gazing down at the river the South Koreans sensed the entire Korean Peninsula was their plum. But their moment of triumph was fleeting. Suddenly thousands of Chinese infantrymen stormed down from the mountain passes and attacked the regiment, killing or capturing two thirds of the men.

Enter the Chinese Army

Like phantoms in the night some 300,000 Chinese soldiers had slipped across the Yalu in the last half of

October and taken up positions in the rugged mountains near the Manchurian border. There they waited for advancing UN troops to fall into carefully laid traps. The Chinese government later claimed these soldiers were "volunteers," but all were members of the regular army. Thirty-three divisions of "volunteers" were poised to throw back UN soldiers. The conflict in Korea was now a new and ever more frightening war.

On the night of November 1, the American 8th Cavalry Regiment was camped north of the city of Unsan. The men were preparing to make a final push to the Yalu and to victory. In the pitch darkness the Americans heard the eerie sound of bugles. The Chinese army had few radios, so their units communicated through bugle refrains. To the GIs, the bugle blasts sounded more like a terror tactic than a method of signaling. After a chilling series of bugle calls the Americans heard shouts and war whoops. Then Chinese troops, in numbers so great their formations disappeared over the horizon, charged into United States lines. The enemy soldiers ran mindlessly, as if they were indifferent to death. After braving machine guns and mortar fire, the Chinese reached American positions and a desperate hand-to-hand struggle broke out. In the cold moonlight men slashed at each other with bayonets and rifle butts, some even hurled stones. One sergeant called the awful combat "cowboy and Indian stuff, only a lot worse." In a score of savage battles the 8th Cavalry Regiment lost more than 600 men.

Word of the massive Chinese intervention echoed along the front. Panic reigned among the Americans as

United States Marines battle Chinese soldiers in North Korea.

rumors flew from outfit to outfit: "The Chinese attack at night. They blow bugles to scare you. There's a million of them out there!" Men who had yet to see a Chinese soldier learned to fear them. "We felt the presence of Chinese all around," said PFC Victor Fox. "We heard stories of them appearing suddenly on all sides, decimating units, then breaking contact and mysteriously fading away."[1]

A strange lull settled over the front in early November. The Americans made few advances; the Chinese, few attacks. Instead both sides felt each other out like boxers in a ring throwing probing punches. Meanwhile raw biting winds howled out of the mountain gorges, and the temperature dropped below freezing. Korea's Arctic-like winter was starting. American troops had no heavy winter clothing because the high command believed the war would be over before cold weather set in. The Chinese, on the other hand, were dressed in quilted field coats to ward off icy winds. In the weeks to come the Americans, acting like scavengers, stripped the jackets off of dead Chinese soldiers and wore them.

Thanksgiving Day, 1950, was celebrated in all American sectors. Men at the front were served turkey with all the trimmings. Most had to eat their dinner in frozen foxholes while cruel winds screamed over their heads. But so what—it was their best meal since arriving in Korea. Unknown to the men, it was also their last day of relative peace.

The lull in combat ended on the night of November 26, as Chinese bugles sounded all along the front. Under

A wounded American soldier waits to be evacuated from the North Korean front.

the cover of darkness, communist troops rushed UN positions in nightmarish suicidal waves. Light artillery and mortars tore into the enemy ranks, but the warriors kept charging over icy terrain. One Marine remembered, "In the first wave everyone would have a weapon. In the second, third, and fourth waves, half wouldn't. They'd pick up a weapon from the guy dead on the ground who didn't need it anymore." American and UN defensive fronts caved in under the brutal assaults.

At the Chosin Reservoir in northeastern Korea, American Marines were knee-deep in snow when they were attacked. "When the Chinese came I was frightened to death," said Sergeant Sherman Richter. "Don't tell me about heroes. Everyone was very afraid."[2] In a confusing battle at the reservoir, the swarming Chinese cut into the rear of Marine positions. The Marines found themselves surrounded, which left them two choices—surrender or death.

The Big Bugout

December 1950 to early January 1951 was a time known to the Americans as "the Big Bugout." *Bugout* is military slang for a hasty retreat. In frozen North Korea, "the Big Bugout" was a frantic six-week period that saw the entire UN front collapse before the Chinese juggernaut. To the men it was the most demoralizing episode of the war. Their October and November offensive had carried them to the promise of victory. The words "home by Christmas" echoed in their thoughts. Now, during "the Big Bugout," they saw territory so painfully gained

A soldier takes cover from the wind and chill in January 1951. At the time, UN forces were battling hordes of Chinese Communist troops.

surrendered to the enemy. And now they wondered when or if this awful war would ever end.

As the troops staggered backward, individuals and units acted heroically to stem the communist tide. Army Corporal Mitchell Red Cloud, a Native American from Wisconsin, was standing guard protecting his company when he was shot and badly wounded by a Chinese patrol. Though the snow beneath him was stained with his blood, Red Cloud pulled himself to his feet, leaned against a tree, and returned fire with his automatic rifle until he was killed. His lonely vigil saved many lives. Red Cloud was posthumously awarded the Congressional Medal of Honor.

The most dramatic struggle of "the Big Bugout" took place at the Chosin Reservoir, where the 1st Marine Division was trapped. Marine officers made the tough decision to fight their way out of the trap by trekking fifty-five miles through enemy-held territory to the port city of Hungnam. At Hungnam the men could be evacuated by sea. From the beginning, the Marines at the Chosin refused to use the word *retreat* to describe their operation since their plans called for a long march into enemy-held territory. One Marine officer said, "Retreat hell, we're simply advancing in another direction."

The Marine break-out began on November 30, 1950. Temperatures had plunged to below 0° Fahrenheit. The bleak Korean landscape supported no large trees as shields against the winds that roared over the hilltops into the ranks of Americans. "It was impossible to describe the cold," said one Marine sergeant. "The

UN trucks take troops and equipment south of the 38th Parallel during the great UN retreat of early 1951.

steel on my rifle was ice. Put bare flesh on it and you stuck, and the only way to get loose was to lose some skin. One time my mouth literally froze shut, my spittle was all frozen and mixed up with my whiskers."

During the long march toward Hungnam the Marines suffered a grim routine. In the daylight hours they hiked, bending into the fierce winds. At night, they fought hordes of Chinese attackers desperate to kill them. Darkness over the Chosin region meant a kaleidoscope of hellish sights and sounds: thumping mortar shells, horrible screams from the wounded and dying, wild bugle blasts, orange tracer bullets arching over the snow.

Of all the units at the Chosin, none suffered worse than Fox Company, 2nd Battalion, 7th Marine Regiment. Fox Company was given the vital task of holding a high hill guarding the Toktong Pass at the division's flank. The Chinese assaulted Fox Company at night, pushing forward to get within hand grenade range. A private named Hector Cafferatta—a man so huge he was nicknamed "Moose" by fellow Marines—began picking up thrown Chinese grenades like a baseball player and hurling them back. One grenade exploded in Cafferatta's grasp, pulverizing the fingers of his right hand. "Moose" Cafferatta later received the Congressional Medal of Honor, the nation's highest award for bravery.

Fox Company's most desperate battle came on its third night in the Chosin region. Again the Chinese attacked in a massed waved formation while bugle calls and battle cries echoed over their ranks. But now the

Marines fought like zombies. They were too exhausted, too cold, too numbed by combat to fear for their lives. For the Chinese the result was carnage. "We let them come into can't-miss range, then opened up," said Fox Company's commander, Captain William Barber. "My God, it was slaughter! The Chinese didn't have a chance."[3]

In their long and painful flight from the Chosin Reservoir, the Marines benefited from overwhelming air power. On either side of the long lines of marchers, American planes bombed and strafed the Chinese. The pilots flew so low men on the ground claimed they saw propellers chop off the limbs of trees. The Marines also received supplies by air drop. And hundreds of badly wounded men and those who had lost fingers or toes to frostbite were airlifted to hospitals from a makeshift field at the town of Hagaru near the reservoir.

By December 14, the great march to Hungnam was completed. More than 100,000 men—Marines, soldiers, and South Korean troops—boarded Navy LSTs and were taken to safety at sea. The Navy also evacuated thousands of hungry and half-frozen civilians. The escape from the Chosin Reservoir is now regarded as one of the epic battles of the Korean War. The Americans lost 3,000 soldiers and twice that number were wounded. The frostbite cases were countless. During the struggle to break out of the Chosin, heroism became almost commonplace. A total of seventeen Congressional Medals of Honor and seventy Navy Crosses were awarded during the campaign—the most ever for a single battle.

On other fronts the depressing retreat continued. By Christmas Day—the day thousands of Americans hoped they would celebrate at home surrounded by their families—the communist forces had pushed the UN below the 38th Parallel. All of North Korea was once more in communist hands.

Ridgway and the Counteroffensive

Since the early months of the war, General MacArthur conducted the overall operations from his headquarters in Tokyo, while General Walton Walker had charge of the battlefront. On December 22, 1950, Walker drove out of Seoul riding in a jeep. He headed toward a battlefront ceremony where he was slated to present several medals, including a Silver Star to his son Captain Sam Walker, a company commander. Halfway to his destination, his jeep was slowed behind a traffic jam of South Korean army trucks. Walker, who was always in a hurry, ordered his driver to veer around the traffic. The driver pulled left and discovered a truck racing at them head on. The jeep swerved off the road and tumbled into a ditch. General Walker was killed in the accident.

In faraway Washington, D.C., General Matthew Ridgway was having dinner with a friend when he received an emergency telephone call. The caller ordered him to report immediately to General MacArthur and take charge of the fighting fronts in Korea. Ridgway excused himself from the table, packed a bag, and boarded a plane for the war zone.

Ridgway was a tough and experienced officer. In

A mother and her three children return to the ruins of their home in
Seoul.

World War II he commanded the 82nd Airborne Division through the thick of combat in France and Germany. Handsome and athletic-looking, he was the picture of a field commander. One associate said of him, "Ridgway reminded me of Superman. You had the impression he could knock over a building with a single blow, or stare a hole in the wall if he wanted to."

Arriving in Korea on December 26, 1950, Ridgway took charge of a thoroughly demoralized Army. On his first day in command he saw his troops trudging backward in steady retreat. He called the scene, ". . . a dismaying spectacle. Soldiers were streaming south without order, without arms, without leaders."[4] Seoul fell to the enemy on January 4, 1951. It seemed that nothing could stop the UN collapse. Ridgway was appalled to hear American officers making plans to pull back all the way to the old Pusan Perimeter.

Ridgway dismissed all ideas of a long retreat. Instead he urged his fellow officers to take the offensive. But before the UN forces could move forward again, the general had to instill fighting spirit among the ranks. "Fighting spirit," he later wrote, "is not something that can be described or spelled out. An experienced commander can feel it through all his senses, in the posture, the manner, the talk, the very gestures of his men."[5] At once, Ridgway changed the little things that were vital to improve morale. He used helicopters to speed up the process of getting letters from home to the men up front. He put field kitchens closer to the lines, making hot chow available to outfits in combat. He scolded his

General Matthew Ridgway (without the sunglasses) seated in a jeep with General Douglas MacArthur (front seat) and General Doyle Hickey (rear seat). This photo was taken near the 38th parallel on April 3, 1951.

commanders for being too "road bound" when planning their attacks. After all, he told them, the communists attacked over open fields instead of exclusively on roads, so the Americans should be able to do the same.

Ridgway's forces were outnumbered about two to one against the communists, but the UN possessed overwhelming superiority in tanks and artillery. Ridgway ordered every artillery piece in the rear echelons to be moved to the front. Even disabled tanks were towed forward so their guns could be trained on the enemy. Massed artillery turned back the enemy's terrible waves of human assaults, leaving ghastly piles of Chinese bodies on the battlefields. Under Ridgway there was no retreat to the Pusan Perimeter. Instead, the communists managed to push the UN forces only 30 or 40 miles south of the 38th Parallel. The cost in Chinese and North Korean lives was tremendous.

On January 25, 1951, Ridgway ordered his officers to launch a general offensive. In contrast to the dazzling break-out following the Inchon landing, this advance was slow and steady. Ridgway insisted the entire front line, spanning the waist of Korea, move forward as a unit. On February 28, UN forces reached the Han River. On March 14, they recaptured Seoul. It was the fourth time the battle lines passed through the devastated South Korean capital. The citizens of Seoul were too dazed and demoralized by warfare to cheer their liberators.

By mid-April 1951, the Ridgway-led UN army had established a wavering defensive line just north of the 38th

Marines take cover behind a tank during a firefight in the spring of 1951.

Parallel. Communist troops began a major counteroffensive on April 17, with the intention of recapturing Seoul. But by this time the UN forces were well entrenched and stopped the enemy. Now a new and frustrating stage—stalemate—settled over the war in Korea.

Stalemate

In chess, a stalemate occurs when the two players realize neither can win the game, and both agree to quit. Stalemate conditions also develop in warfare. But war is a far deadlier game than chess, and it is never easy for the two sides to simply quit and walk away from the table.

Early in 1951, American political leaders had begun to consider the war in Korea to be unwinnable. Even if the UN forces were to advance deeper into North Korea, the politicians feared the Chinese communists would simply send in more troops and start a drive of their own. In order to overcome Chinese power, the Americans would have to pour thousands of men into Korea, and perhaps expand the war beyond the Yalu River by bombing bases in Manchuria and China proper. In Washington, President Truman and his advisers believed the American public would not support a wider war. So instead of pressing farther north, American leaders decided to hold the present line near the 38th Parallel and look for a face-saving way out of Korea.

Many military men disagreed with Washington's course of stalemate. A principal figure among the dissenters was General Douglas MacArthur. "In war there is no substitute for victory," MacArthur thundered.

Newspapers quoted him, denouncing the politicians for their defeatist attitudes and urging his Washington bosses to strike targets north of the Yalu River. He even hinted the atomic bomb should be used to vanquish Red China. The general's tough talk led to a bitter clash between him and President Truman.

Unlike MacArthur, General Matthew Ridgway reluctantly accepted the stalemate that developed on the Korean front. Years after the war Ridgway wrote:

> We could have pushed right on to the Yalu in the spring of 1951. But the price for such a drive would have been far too high for what we would have gained. We would have lost heavily in dead and wounded—my estimate at the time was 100,000. . . . Would [the American people] underwrite the bloody cost of [such a] campaign? Would they commit themselves to an endless war in the bottomless pit of the Asian mainland? I thought then and I think now that the answer to these questions was, "No."[6]

"If the best minds in the world set out to find the worst possible location in the world to fight this damnable war, politically and militarily, the unanimous choice would be Korea."
—Dean Acheson, secretary of state under Harry Truman.

5 Issues Beyond the Battlefield

Government workers often complain their bosses tend to "pass the buck," let someone else make the tough decisions. President Truman disdained this tendency in government. On his desk at the White House sat a sign proclaiming, "The Buck Stops Here." On April 11, 1951, he made one of the toughest decisions of his presidency. He fired Douglas MacArthur, the supreme commander of UN forces in Korea.

Truman Fires MacArthur

"Truman Fires Mac" blared a headline in the *Chicago Tribune*. "Mac Gets Sacked" declared another paper's headline. News of MacArthur's dismissal stunned the American people. He was the most famous soldier of the

twentieth century. He had served in the Army for fifty-
two years, and won a Congressional Medal of Honor in
World War II. How could the president summarily oust
such a universally respected military figure?

But the president blamed MacArthur for the frustrating events in Korea. Even many of MacArthur's fellow
generals held him responsible for the war's reversals. He
had crossed the 38th Parallel on faulty intelligence, be-
lieving the Chinese army would stay out of the conflict.
He split his forces in the rugged North Korean mountains, making it easier for the Chinese to drive the UN
troops backward. Many military insiders believed the un-
expected Chinese entry into the war had confused and
dismayed MacArthur, rendering him unfit to command.
Author William Manchester, who wrote a best-selling bi-
ography of MacArthur, said, "We shall never know what
was in MacArthur's mind that terrible winter after the
Chinese came into the war. This much seems certain: he
had lost his fighting spirit."[1]

Worst of all, MacArthur turned on Truman, blam-
ing him for the stalemate situation in Korea. To
newspaper writers, the general said he needed freedom to
bomb targets in communist China. Only by attacking
China could he bring the war to an end and destroy
Asian communism in the process. Actually, President
Truman was using the stalemate as an opportunity to
send peace feelers to China. MacArthur knew this, and
he circumvented Truman's efforts by offering China
peace on his terms. His terms were far more severe than

Mrs. Roosevelt talks with President Truman. Truman hoped the stalemate in Korea would bring the war to an end.

Truman's. The general threatened to destroy China unless it surrendered.

MacArthur's intervention in the delicate peace negotiations with China infuriated the president. Also, MacArthur had made speeches and written letters to key politicians, denouncing Truman's conduct of the war. The President decided enough was enough. He had taken all the insubordination he intended to take from the general. The U.S. Constitution gives the president supreme authority over the military. Hero or not, MacArthur was fired. The buck had stopped.

After his dismissal, MacArthur returned to the United States where he was greeted as a hero. Truman's political enemies portrayed MacArthur as a miracle worker who could end the war in Korea if only the president would untie his hands. His military mistakes in Korea were momentarily forgotten. His defiance of the president and of the Constitution were also forgotten. It became unpatriotic—indeed unAmerican—to find fault with the general.

MacArthur's shining hour came on April 19, 1951, eight days after his dismissal, when he gave an address before a joint session of Congress. The entire country was strangely silent as the speech was broadcast coast to coast via radio. The address was even sent into high school and grade school classrooms. Thirty times during his thirty-four-minute speech, the general had to halt as Congressmen cheered until they were hoarse. In tears at the end, MacArthur recalled the words to a barracks' ballad popular near the turn of the century when he served

General MacArthur addresses a joint session of Congress on April 19, 1951. President Truman fired MacArthur for interfering in the peace negotiations with China. Behind him are Vice-President Albin Barkley (left) and House Speaker Sam Rayburn.

as a junior officer. "[The song] proclaimed most proudly that old soldiers never die, they just fade away. And like the old soldier of that ballad, I now close my military career and just fade away, an old soldier who tried to do his duty as God gave him the right to see that duty. Goodbye."

In Korea, General Matthew Ridgway was given MacArthur's former job and took over his offices in Tokyo. Lieutenant General James Van Fleet took charge of the ground operations. At the front, bitter battles were fought, but neither side achieved a dramatic breakthrough into the other's territory. Americans, meanwhile, tried to carry on their daily lives while the suffering and killing in Korea dragged on and on.

The Forgotten War

In late June 1951, American troops began what their leaders termed a "limited offensive." Given the static nature of the battle lines, no high-ranking officer wanted to use the words "full offensive." The object of the American advance was a region just above the 38th Parallel called the Iron Triangle, an area bounded by the cities of Pyongyang, Chorwon, and Kumhwa. Fighting in the Iron Triangle was savage. American attacks were met with determined communist counterattacks. By the first week in July, the 1st Marine Regiment alone suffered sixty men killed and hundreds more wounded.

Despite the terrible bloodletting, the battle for the Iron Triangle received little mention in the American press. *Life* dedicated its early July issue to the launching

South Korean soldiers pose amid the ruins of a village.

of the U.S.S. *United States,* a luxury liner. *Newsweek* did not cover the battle at all. All major magazines and newspapers paid considerable attention to a June 23 radio broadcast by Jacob Malik, the Russian ambassador to the UN. In the broadcast, Malik urged a cease-fire and peace negotiations in Korea. This was welcome news; it offered the country a chance to escape the awful mess in that land. War news was less inviting. Few Americans wanted to read about battles where scores of men were killed over a few miles of dreary landscape.

In the minds of Americans, the Korean War was a drama in two acts. At first, Americans cheered President Truman's decision to send troops to Korea. It was time, the people thought, to get tough with the communists and stop their aggression. The Inchon landings and the electrifying offensive into North Korea renewed Americans' faith in their military might. Then the Chinese intervened and the depressing second act began. As the war entered a crippling no-win stage, the audience lost interest in the show.

By July 1951, the Korean War was a year old. Already it had caused 69,000 American battle casualties. To the American public, the battle lines had a dispiriting "yo-yo" syndrome—we take a few miles of real estate one day; they take it back the next. The people at home rejected this brand of warfare. Only six years earlier the country fought and defeated both Germany and Japan. Campaigns in that war provided excitement as Americans followed battle action in newspapers while their soldiers pressed ever closer to the enemy's heartland. By contrast, the stalemate in Korea was dismal reading.

Also, Korea was an undeclared war. It was fought by orders of the president rather than by a vote from Congress. This was a different war, a limited war, and one that Americans disdained fighting.

The American people coped with the Korean War by ignoring it. The writer William Manchester reported, "People at home stopped following news about the war. Suspecting that literally no one was reading about it any more, an Oregon newspaper ran one war story two days in a row—same text . . . and not one single subscriber noticed the repetition."[2] Korea became "the Forgotten War," a term historians use to describe it to this day. It was snubbed at home after the stalemate stage developed, and even today it receives scant attention in many history books.

When peace talks began in the summer of 1951, urgent news came from the diplomatic rather than the military front. Politicians argued endlessly over what the nation's policy should be at the peace table. Government leaders hoped to get the country out of the war, but in the process they wanted to mask any suggestion of defeat or surrender to the communists. Of course the men at the battlefronts had no time to ponder the peace negotiations. They were desperately trying to stay alive in a war whose violence never ceased. As a Marine named Jack Orth put it, "The scuttlebutt [rumor] of an armistice was rampant, but no one bothered to tell the Chinese. They

United States soldiers shield themselves from exploding mortar shells. Although Korea was one of the bloodiest wars in history, the American people largely ignored it.

seemed to intensify their shelling and attacks up and down the line."[3]

The War and Presidential Politics

"I'm going to have a Truman beer; it's just like any other beer except it doesn't have a head on it." "You know the war wouldn't have happened if Truman were alive." These and other cruel "Truman jokes" made the rounds from neighborhood to neighborhood in 1951 and 1952. The United States was caught in a war it could not win and from which it could not withdraw, free from disgrace. And the public believed this terrible situation was brought about by Harry Truman's bungling. The president was burned in effigy in Oklahoma and in Kansas. Flags were flown upside down in many parts of the country to signal national emergency. In Congress there was open talk of impeaching the president.

Regular presidential elections were scheduled in November 1952. Only a few diehard Democrats wanted Harry Truman to run again. Polls showed just one in four Americans approved of him as their leader. Instead the Democrats gravitated toward Adlai Stevenson, the witty and intellectual governor of Illinois. Stevenson was handicapped in that he had to defend the unpopular war policies of Truman, his fellow Democrat. Also Stevenson had no concrete program for pulling the nation out of the Korean conflict.

The Republicans sensed victory. For nineteen years, under Franklin D. Roosevelt and Truman, a Democrat had occupied the White House. Now the unpopular

Korean War threw the presidency up for grabs. Many Republicans wanted to see Douglas MacArthur head their party and run for the office. But the fame MacArthur commanded after his dismissal had waned.

Congressional hearings held in May and June 1951 again exposed the fact that MacArthur had defied Truman's orders and thereby violated the Constitution. The hearings also revealed that other high-ranking generals, including the honored World War II leader Omar Bradley, agreed with Truman's decision to fire MacArthur.

As their presidential choice the Republicans turned to Dwight Eisenhower, another esteemed World War II general. Eisenhower, who was often affectionately called by his nickname "Ike," had no political allegiances. It was not known if he voted Democrat or Republican, or indeed, if he voted at all. He was respected as a man of decency and strength, and after much persuasion by Republican leaders he agreed to run. His early campaign speeches were flat, and the election was in doubt. Then, on October 24 in Detroit, Eisenhower delivered a master stroke when he promised to bring the war in Korea to an early and honorable end. "That job," he said, "requires a personal trip to Korea. I shall make that trip. Only that way can I learn best how to serve the American people in the cause of peace. I shall go to Korea."

Eisenhower's speech created a sensation. The dark presence of the Korean War was on everyone's mind, even if people were uncomfortable reading about it in the newspapers. Now "Ike" had promised to bring it to a conclusion. He did not elaborate how his visit would deliver peace. But his pledge alone was enough to excite national hope. Campaign posters blared out the message "Bring the boys home, Ike."

Adlai Stevenson and the Democrats denounced Eisenhower's proposed trip as nothing more than a campaign gimmick. Always the humorist, Stevenson quipped, "If elected, I shall go to the White House." However, Stevenson was unable to offer even the hope of a quick end to the Korean War. In November, Eisenhower won a landslide victory.

One issue not mentioned in the presidential campaigns was the possible use of nuclear weapons to break the deadlock in Korea. MacArthur had advocated hitting targets in communist China with the atomic bomb, but most world leaders dismissed the general's comments as saber-rattling. In a November 1950 press conference, Truman said he was ready to go after communist China with "every weapon we have." He thereby implied a nuclear threat. Truman's words caused a furor in Britain and France. The Soviet Union had exploded its first A-bomb in 1949. America's European allies feared the Korean War could widen to a nuclear conflict between the two superpowers, with Europe a primary battleground. After Truman's press conference, American leaders confined their discussions of nuclear weapons in Korea to closed-door conferences.

Korean Civilians and Refugees

They crammed the roads, slept amid ruins, and ate from garbage pits. These people were the refugees. No one

Dwight Eisenhower reacts to bad news during World War II. Later as part of his presidential campaign, Eisenhower would promise to visit Korea to see if he could end that war.

knew their precise number, but it was estimated that the war turned at least three million Koreans into drifting nomads. Their farms, villages, and cities lay in ruins. Some 600,000 houses were flattened in the first year of fighting. A UN relief worker said, "I doubt that ever in the history of the world, since perhaps the sacking of Carthage, has there been such complete destruction as there has been in Korea."

The Koreans uprooted by the war seemed to be afflicted with a strange wandering sickness. They trekked aimlessly up and down the roads, hoping only to get as far from the fighting as possible. Veterans of the war will never forget their sea of faces, a picture of misery on the march. General Matthew Ridgway often saw the pathetic processions. "The scenes shall always live in my mind," he wrote, "men, women, and children, patriarchs with storybook beards, grandmothers carried on their sons' backs like children . . . all without a destination except some spot far from the Chinese."[4]

The cruel winter months took a terrible toll on the refugees. Old people and babies were the first to die. Families, too weakened by hunger to bury their dead in the frozen ground, simply let the bodies lay like crumpled dolls along the roadsides.

The refugees were the truly forgotten people in "the Forgotten War." Government and UN agencies provided food for only a fraction of the homeless masses. In fact, the governments of both North and South Korea added to the refugee ranks because their terror tactics forced people to flee their homes and villages. The North

Endless file of refugees streaming over snow swept fields during the winter of 1950 to 1951.

Korean army routinely slaughtered South Koreans who even remotely opposed their regime. The greatest mass killing of the war took place at Taejon, South Korea. There the North Koreans executed 5,000 to 7,000 civilians and dumped their bodies into a shallow trench. The grisly collective grave was discovered by UN troops who recaptured Taejon shortly after the shootings.

One refugee, driven from his home by fear of the North Koreans, was thirteen-year-old Suk Bun Yoon of Seoul. The boy watched in the first week of the war as communist soldiers marched into Seoul and immediately plastered large posters of Joseph Stalin and Kim Il Sung on the buildings. The Yoon family was forced to hide in the basement of a bombed-out house. Yoon's father owned a small store. Because he was a merchant, the communists denounced him as "an enemy of the people." The family managed to escape from Seoul and then spent the rest of the war traveling with hordes of refugees. Once, while in the company of hundreds of other homeless people, they crossed a frozen river as a battle raged nearby. Shell fire shattered the ice under their feet and thirteen-year-old Yoon watched in horror as scores of refugees plunged to their deaths in the frigid waters.

The South Korean government also brutalized the civilian population in occupied North Korea and at home. Syngman Rhee and his lieutenants were fanatical in their desire to unify the country under his rule. Anyone whom they accused of working with the communists was executed. Rhee's treatment of defenseless civilians was a source of constant embarrassment to America and its

South Korean civilians weep over the bodies of loved ones, many of whom were killed while being held captive by the North Korean army.

allies. A British soldier wrote to his superior officer claiming he saw, "Forty emaciated and subdued Koreans taken about a mile from where I was stationed and shot [by the South Korean army] while their hands were tied behind them. The whole incident has caused ill feeling among the men of my unit. Our troops are wondering which side in Korea is right." Hundreds of similar incidents were reported by UN soldiers and brought to Rhee's attention. Always, the South Korean president denied there was any wrongdoing in his government.

Month by month the conditions faced by the refugees worsened. In January 1951, *Newsweek* reported:

> The cost of carrying on [the war] in Korea as told in terms of human misery includes: the Korean refugee women whom British soldiers stopped from tossing their infants into an icy creek . . . the thousands sheltered in stinking cattle pens and in packing box crates . . . the dirty, ugly city of Pusan swarming with one million people, twice the normal population . . . the refugee woman giving birth by the roadside of whom [an American officer reported], "She just threw the baby into a ditch. What could we do?"[5]

Nam Il, the communist peace negotiator: "Have you come here to negotiate for peace or just to look for a continuation of the war?"
Admiral C. Turner Joy, the UN peace negotiator: "I object to your rude, discourteous, and immature remarks!"

—A typical exchange between diplomats at the peace table, this one taking place July 28, 1951, at Kaesong.

6 The Final Two Years

 In the summer of 1951, the events in Korea were two-staged: diplomats talked peace while soldiers waged war. Peace talks began on July 10 at the city of Kaesong, but no cease-fire arrangement accompanied the discussions. Consequently the war continued to rage in all its deadly intensity. This frustrating situation of peace negotiations taking place in the middle of furious combat continued for the next two years. And the violence of the war did not diminish during the armistice discussions. Combat casualties for both sides were greater in the period after the peace talks began than they were before the negotiations.

Despite the frenzy of warfare it seemed in 1951 that

General Nam Il and other Chinese delegates make their way to the
peace talks in Kaesong.

the time for peace in Korea had come. The Russians wanted to end the hostilities, as did the Americans and the Chinese. But when the negotiations commenced, dozens of squabbles erupted at the conference table. Many of the disagreements were petty. Admiral C. Turner Joy, the chief American negotiator, objected to the fact he was assigned a chair with unusually short legs, allowing the Chinese delegate to tower over him. Nam Il, the Chinese arbitrator, insisted Chinese troops in Korea be called "volunteers" instead of soldiers. The thorniest issue dividing the delegates when the talks started was the Chinese demand that all armies pull back to the pre-war 38th Parallel. Battle lines at this point were mostly north of the parallel, and the Americans refused to give up hard-won ground. On the 38th Parallel issue the negotiators lost their tempers, shouting matches broke out, and the talks were temporarily suspended on August 23.

"The War of the Hills"

While the delegates stormed at each other, a particularly punishing period called the "War of the Hills" developed on the front. Each side wanted to take certain key hills in hopes of improving its position at the peace table. Terrible battles raged over rocky outcroppings that the Americans nicknamed Porkchop Hill, Heartbreak Ridge, Old Baldy, and Bloody Ridge. Communist troops dug an intricate network of trenches and tunnels into these high grounds. Fighting during the "War of the Hills" took on the nightmare quality associated with World

Soldiers battle for key positions in the "War of the Hills."

War I trench lines. As an army PFC named Troy Hamm reported:

> There was this one particular bunker, on Hill 602, that we fired at all day. Artillery and air strikes were called in. Again and again we destroyed this bunker, and again and again [they] rebuilt it. By sundown it had been leveled to the ground, and we could no longer see it. . . . [From the bunker] the enemy fired at us. At one point I smelled exploded powder and an odor that was new to me. An incoming round had made a direct hit on one of the guys, and pieces of him were scattered all over the area.[1]

From their hillside fortresses the Chinese launched fearsome assaults. "The Chinese, of course, delighted to attack at night, when our air power was grounded and our observers blind," wrote General Matthew Ridgway.

> We tried all sorts of [illumination] devices, including powerful searchlights that bounced their glare off low-hanging clouds. . . . The night attacks were as weird and dreamlike as ever, preceded by the unworldly wailing of Chinese bugles . . . designed to chill a westerner's blood.[2]

By the time of the "War of the Hills," seventeen UN countries had contributed troops to the cause. Americans made up 90 percent of the non-Korean allied soldiers; Great Britain was the second largest contributor. Soldiers also came from France, India, Thailand, Turkey, Greece, and other nations. This great international mix created a supply problem. The Dutch troops wanted milk with their meals, while the French demanded wine. The

Hindus could eat no beef; the Muslims, no pork. Bread had to be served to the Europeans and rice to the Asians. Many American soldiers grew to admire the Turkish troops for their showy, sometimes foolhardy, bravery. The Turks regularly gathered around campfires at night and sang songs as if daring the Chinese to attack.

Peace talks resumed on October 25, after a sixty-six-day lapse. Now the talks took place in the city of Panmunjom, where they would be held for the rest of the war. Again the delegates argued, often over trivial issues. The size and positioning of the UN flag as opposed to the Chinese or North Korean flag became a major source of contention.

While the negotiations proceeded, battles in the field often had greater political significance than military aims. In October the communists made a determined attack on White Horse Hill, which was defended primarily by South Korean troops. Chinese prisoners later confessed the offensive was designed to coincide with the American elections in November. The enemy hoped a dramatic reversal on the battlefront would disgust Americans and make them demand peace at any price from their leaders. But the Chinese failed miserably in their attempt to take the hill. They lost some 10,000 soldiers, and American voters—uninterested in war news anyway—were not affected by their efforts.

As he promised, President-elect Dwight Eisenhower visited Korea on December 2, 1952. He chatted with American troops, including his son John, who was serving in the Army as an officer. But Eisenhower could

The bleak meeting place at Panmunjom where peace talks were held.

offer no hope of concluding the war soon. To news reporters he said, "How difficult it seems to be in a war of this kind to work out a plan that would bring a positive end and definite victory without possibly running the grave risk of enlarging the war."

Meanwhile the cycle of fighting and talking continued—seemingly without end.

The Air War

Early in the Korean conflict the American Air Force enjoyed almost uncontested dominance of the skies. Then on November 8, 1950, American planes flying a mission near the Yalu River were attacked by a squadron of Russian-built MiG jets. The MiG-15 was a sleek, swept-wing fighter with a top speed of 670 mph—a full 100 mph faster than any American plane in Korea at the time. Amazingly an American F-80 jet fighter managed to shoot down one of the attacking MiGs. It was history's first jet against jet aerial dogfight. And that one encounter changed the nature of the Korean air war.

The sudden emergence of the MiG forced the Americans to rush their newest fighter, the F-86 Saber, to Korea. Both the MiG and the Saber owed their designs to World War II German engineers who were the first to fly jet fighter planes with sharply swept-back wings. Consequently the Saber and the MiG were similar in appearance, size, and speed. Only the experience and quality training of American pilots allowed them to prevail in the air war. Most MiGs were flown by Chinese and North Koreans who lacked training time in the

The MiG-15, a superb Russian-built jet fighter flown mainly by
Chinese pilots.

high-performance jets. The Americans, on the other hand, had hundreds of hours in Sabers. Also many of the American pilots were veterans of World War II aerial combat. The result was an aerial massacre. Over the skies of Korea the Sabers shot down seventeen MiGs for every one American jet lost in combat.

Most dogfights took place in "MiG Alley," a region just south of the Yalu River. The MiGs took off from airbases in China, which they regarded as a safe haven. American pilots were forbidden to cross the Yalu because their leaders believed such an intrusion would widen the war.

Saber pilots were heroes to their fellow pilots and to the ground crews. The most celebrated "jet jockey" was Captain Joseph McConnell, an Air Force pilot since World War II. His wingman said, "McConnell would start shooting at planes only he could see. A thousand, twelve hundred yards off—range didn't mean a thing to him. He'd open up, and before you knew it he'd start getting hits. 'If you get one shot in on the turbine,' he would say, 'the enemy is going to start losing power. . . . If you shoot off a blade, you've got him.' "[3] Before his service was up McConnell had shot down sixteen MiGs, to become America's greatest "ace" pilot in the Korean air war.

Now and then the Sabers would encounter a MiG flown by an enemy pilot who showed extraordinary ability. The Americans suspected these superior pilots were Russians, using the Korean War to gain combat experience in jets. Russian government leaders hotly denied

The American F-86 Saber jet, the UN's answer to the MiG-15.

any of their men were flying the MiGs, but the Americans believed differently. "I remember a day," said Air Force Colonel Robert Baldwin, "when one of our people shot down a MiG and the pilot bailed out. I flew near to have a look and there he was, hanging in the air from his parachute, red hair just shining in the sun. I don't think there were that many red-headed Chinese or North Koreans."[4]

During the "War of the Hills," General Ridgway ordered a stepped up aerial offensive, hoping constant bombing would soften the enemy's resistance. The new air war amounted to a scorched-earth campaign. Nothing was spared, including civilian housing. Massive B-29s, the most powerful bomber of World War II, pounded North Korean cities. The North Korean capital of Pyongyang was one of many cities flattened by repeated B-29 raids. Thousands of Pyongyang civilians were killed, and those who survived dug deep shelters below the city's ruins and lived the miserable existence of cave dwellers.

Fighter bombers dropping napalm—the searing jellied gasoline bombs—wreaked the greatest havoc. An American newspaper writer named George Barrett entered a village near the front and gave a chilling picture of napalm's aftermath:

> A napalm raid hit the village three or four days ago [and nobody] buried the dead because there is nobody left to do so. This correspondent came across one old woman, the only one who seemed to be left alive, dazedly hanging up some clothes

in a blackened courtyard filled with the bodies of her family. The inhabitants throughout the villages were caught and killed, and kept the exact postures they held when the napalm struck—a man about to get on his bicycle; fifty or so boys and girls playing at an orphanage . . . there must be two hundred dead in the tiny hamlet.[5]

Despite the horror brought from the skies, the bombing offensive had little effect on the "War of the Hills." The front stayed roughly the same, and at the negotiating table neither side was willing to budge.

The POWs

Topping the list of problems at the peace table was the future of the prisoners of war. When peace negotiations began, the UN held 171,000 POWs in various South Korean camps. Routine questioning of these prisoners revealed that about 50,000 of them hated living under communism and did not want to go home when they were set free. At the negotiating table the United States insisted prisoners be given the right to choose where they wanted to go upon their release. The "turncoat" POWs were an embarrassment to the communists. They demanded all captives be returned to their country of origin regardless of their wishes. The communists also managed to extend the war into the prison camps by placing agitators in a huge POW facility on Koje Island in South Korea. The agitators sparked a civil war between pro- and anti-communist POWs.

From the beginning of the war, prisoners on both sides faced a grim fate. When it was inconvenient for the

North Korean army to march prisoners to camps behind the lines, they simply murdered them. The American public was outraged in October 1950, when the bodies of almost one hundred American POWs were found shot in a North Korean railroad tunnel. A few men survived by feigning death. They told the horrible story of being cut down by machine gun fire as they waited in a chow line.

The Chinese subjected prisoners to "brainwashing," a brutal form of persuasion. During brainwashing sessions, prisoners were questioned and lectured to for hours while being forced to stand at attention and denied food and sleep. An American doctor who examined the victims said, "Brainwashing brought a man to a point where a dry crust off bread or a few hours of uninterrupted sleep became a great event in his life." The goal of brainwashing was to convert prisoners to communism, or to compel them to sign confessions stating they had committed war crimes. For the most part the brainwashing techniques failed. After the war only twenty-one Americans elected to stay in North Korea or China and live under communism. Others, however, confessed to "war crimes."

The most highly publicized war-crime accusation was that American planes had dropped disease-carrying fleas, ticks, and mosquitoes on North Korean cities. The charges were delivered after a terrible influenza epidemic swept North Korea and China during the winter of 1951 to 1952. Rampaging epidemics had long been common in Asia, especially during the winter months. The United

Chinese and North Korean prisoners assembled at a POW camp near Pusan, South Korea.

States denounced the germ warfare indictment as propaganda. The International Red Cross offered to send scientists to the region to investigate the charges, but North Korea refused to let Red Cross representatives enter their country. Still the communists insisted the United States had engaged in bacterial warfare that resulted in thousands of civilian deaths. They based their accusations on thirty-nine confessions obtained from American POW pilots and flight crews. All of the prisoners who signed the confessions had been subjected to brainwashing.

Peace at Last

By the spring of 1953, the political and military leadership of the Korean War had changed. Matthew Ridgway was transferred to Europe and General Mark Clark took his place in Asia. Eisenhower was now the American president. Most significant, on March 5, 1953, the Russian premier Joseph Stalin died.

Historians still question the extent to which the Soviet Union orchestrated the Korean War. At the time, Americans assumed all communist countries followed Moscow's lead. The belief in a worldwide communist monolith directed by Russia dominated American thinking during the Cold War years. Today it is known the Russians had far less influence over the Korean conflict than many Americans believed in the early 1950s. Still, after Stalin's death, communist demands at the peace table softened and the talks proceeded at a swifter pace.

The first breakthrough at Panmunjom came when

Three Americans rest after being released from a Chinese POW camp. Many Chinese captors tried to "brainwash" or persuade their prisoners to convert to communism.

the two sides agreed upon a prisoner exchange arrangement called Operation Little Switch. In April 1953, the UN turned over 6,670 sick and wounded communist prisoners in exchange for 684 UN prisoners—including 149 Americans. Operation Little Switch infuriated South Korean President Syngman Rhee. The South Korean leader was a diehard who insisted the UN accept no peace with the communists. On June 18, Syngman Rhee shocked UN leaders by ordering the release of 25,000 anti-communist POWs from South Korean camps. The sudden release angered the communists and set back the mood of the talks.

But the negotiations now had a momentum of their own, defying the South Korean president's attempt to sabotage their progress. The communists agreed on a major prisoner exchange, called Operation Big Switch, which gave repatriated prisoners a choice of their destiny. Under provisions of Operation Big Switch, those prisoners who refused to return to a communistic system would be turned over to a commission composed of neutral countries. Communist officers would be allowed to give the rebellious POWs "political lectures" aimed at persuading them to return to the communist fold. If they still refused, the commission would repatriate them to non-communist countries. The communists also agreed to establish a demilitarized zone 2.5 miles (4 kilometers) wide running along the present battle lines. The demilitarized zone would serve as the future border between North and South Korea.

The war continued, bloody and thundering to its last

A UN soldier seeks his enemy. The last major Chinese offensive was driven back by massive UN artillery.

gasps. In June 1953, when final agreement was near, the communists launched a major offensive against a bulge in the line held by South Koreans. General Mark Clark said the Chinese merely wanted to give the South Koreans "a bloody nose" before peace became a reality. The Chinese offensive was driven back by massed UN artillery. June was the last full month of fighting, but during this month, the UN fired 2.7 million rounds of artillery shells—the highest monthly total expended during the entire Korean conflict!

At last both sides announced a cease-fire and an armistice signing ceremony to take place on July 27. Up to the final hour, combat continued at the front. "Those last few days were mighty rough," said a Marine from the 1st Division. "Each time we thought the war was over, we'd have to go out and fight again. I had a good buddy killed on the last day."

At 10:00 A.M. on July 27, 1953, diplomats and generals from both sides drove to a meeting spot at Panmunjom to sign the peace documents. Even as the men approached the table, sporadic artillery bursts rumbled in the background. In a brief and businesslike manner, representatives of the UN and the communists signed the papers. There were no handshakes, not even a smile or a wink. No delegate from South Korea was present because Syngman Rhee refused to sign the armistice. He did, however, agree to respect its terms.

Over the 1st Marine Division's sector, red smoke streamers burst in the sky. This was the agreed-upon signal to begin the cease-fire. Still the artillery did not

American and Chinese negotiators meet at Panmunjom.

stop instantly. The booming reports merely faded away, like a summer storm. Finally silence prevailed. What a strange, what a pleasant sensation. Marines were able to hear each other cough and sneeze—and even yawn.

That night a full moon glowed orange and cool above what had been a frantic battlefront only days earlier. Now the strangest sound of all drifted over the Marines' foxholes—singing. It came from the Chinese lines. The Chinese troops were singing, hoarse and off-key, but the joy in their voices was unmistakable. A few surprised Marines, not knowing what else to do, returned the courtesy by singing the Marine Corps Hymn.

Peace.

"I swear, I broke down and cried. I wanted to get out of that place [Korea] so bad that I cried when I finally got on that ship."
—An American soldier remembering his departure from war-torn Korea.

7 Legacy of "The Forgotten War"

 Upon signing the armistice documents General Mark Clark, the commander in Korea, said, "I cannot find it in me to exult at this moment." With those words, Clark expressed feelings shared by the vast majority of his countrymen. Americans breathed a collective sigh of relief. No longer would men and women have to die and suffer in a land thousands of miles from American shores. But there were no victory parades at home. Unlike World War II, the Korean conflict did not end in victory; it simply ended.

Loss of life after three years of warfare was appalling. The American death toll stood at 54,246. More than two million Koreans, most of them civilians, died. The

Chinese government never released its casualty figures, but it is estimated that Chinese forces suffered about one million deaths. Property damage was beyond estimation. From the Yalu River south to Pusan, the two Koreas lay in ruins. Korea was one of the most destructive wars in all history.

Despite the tragic war, the Korean political situation was largely unchanged. The peninsula remained divided into two politically opposite and mutually hostile countries. The demilitarized zone, which snaked along the width of Korea just north of the old 38th Parallel, marked the border between North Korea and South Korea. The new border gave South Korea about 1,500 square miles of territory it did not possess before the war. That tiny gain could never offset the terrible cost of warfare.

In the 1990s, the 151-mile-long demilitarized zone still serves as the border between north and south. Now, more than forty years after the armistice, shell craters, trenches, and other reminders of war can still be seen scarring the land that separates the two countries. And even today, the threat of renewed war between North and South Korea is ever present. By 1994, many nuclear experts agreed that North Korea would soon have all of the necessary materials to build several atomic bombs, if they had not done so already. Possession of such a weapon would surely upset the delicate military balance between the two countries.

On the positive side, the Korean War marked the first time in history a world organization acted in concert

The Korean War

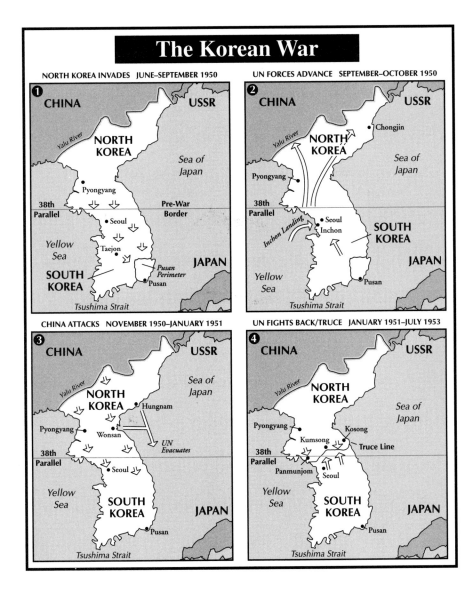

NORTH KOREA INVADES   JUNE–SEPTEMBER 1950

① CHINA · USSR · NORTH KOREA · Yalu River · Sea of Japan · Pyongyang · 38th Parallel · Pre-War Border · Seoul · Yellow Sea · Taejon · JAPAN · Pusan Perimeter · Pusan · SOUTH KOREA · Tsushima Strait

UN FORCES ADVANCE   SEPTEMBER–OCTOBER 1950

② CHINA · USSR · NORTH KOREA · Chongjin · Yalu River · Sea of Japan · Pyongyang · 38th Parallel · Seoul · Inchon · Inchon Landing · SOUTH KOREA · Yellow Sea · JAPAN · Pusan · Tsushima Strait

CHINA ATTACKS   NOVEMBER 1950–JANUARY 1951

③ CHINA · USSR · Sea of Japan · NORTH KOREA · Yalu River · Hungnam · Pyongyang · Wonsan · UN Evacuates · 38th Parallel · Seoul · Yellow Sea · SOUTH KOREA · JAPAN · Pusan · Tsushima Strait

UN FIGHTS BACK/TRUCE   JANUARY 1951–JULY 1953

④ CHINA · USSR · NORTH KOREA · Sea of Japan · Yalu River · Pyongyang · Kosong · Kumsong · Truce Line · 38th Parallel · Panmunjom · Seoul · Yellow Sea · SOUTH KOREA · JAPAN · Pusan · Tsushima Strait

to stop a military aggressor. The strong international response to the North Korean attack surprised communist leaders. Evidence now suggests that top communists, including Russian premier Joseph Stalin, believed the world community would regard the 1950 North Korean assault as the beginning of a minor civil war and allow South Korea to fall to the superior North Korean army. When the United States and the UN came to South Korea's rescue, the communists found they had plunged into a much deeper war than they expected. Some historians believe the UN's strong stand in Korea discouraged the communists from making aggressive moves in other parts of Asia or in Europe, which could have sparked World War III.

The lessons of the Korean War, however, did not prevent the United States from entering another destructive undeclared war in Asia. In the 1960s, about a dozen years after the last shot in Korea was fired, America began sending large numbers of troops to Vietnam. Like Korea, the war in Vietnam began as a civil war between communist and non-communist forces. Also, the war in Vietnam quickly became unpopular at home. But during the Vietnam era, angry Americans took to the streets to demand that their leaders end the conflict and bring the soldiers home. Americans in the 1950s were less inclined to demonstrate against their government. Finally, a comparison of casualty figures from the two wars demonstrates the sheer violence of the Korean conflict. Large-scale American involvement in Vietnam lasted nine years, and some 58,000 American men and women were killed—only about 4,000 more deaths than in Korea, a three-year war.

The 1953 peace in Korea marked an unsatisfactory end to a frustrating war. Yet it meant families around the United States would finally be reunited. One of those families was headed by Dwight Eisenhower, whose son was an Army officer in Korea. The American President said, "We have won an armistice on a single battlefield—not peace in the world. The war is over and I hope my son is going to come home soon."

Around the country thousands of families also waited for sons and daughters to come home.

Chronology

August 8, 1945—The Soviet Union declared war against Japan.

August 9, 1945—The Soviet Union began a powerful offensive against Japanese-held territory in Manchuria, just north of Korea.

August 11, 1945—Soviet troops entered Korea.

August 14, 1945—Japan surrendered to the United States and its Allies.

September 2, 1945—The Russian army halted its advance in Korea at the 38th Parallel. This was in compliance with an agreement drawn up in Washington D.C., that allowed Russian troops to occupy North Korea and American troops to occupy South Korea. The divided Korea arrangement was supposed to be temporary.

August 15, 1948—The government of South Korea, named the Republic of Korea, was officially formed.

September 9, 1948—The government of North Korea, the Democratic People's Republic of Korea, was established.

June 25, 1950—The North Korean army invaded South Korea.

June 27, 1950—The UN Security Council condemned the North Korean attack and asked member states to come to South Korea's assistance.

June 28, 1950—Seoul fell to the North Korean army.

June 29, 1950—President Harry Truman authorized the sending of United States ground forces to Korea.

July 5, 1950—Task Force Smith, an advance group composed of 400 American soldiers, clashed with the North Koreans near the town of Osan.

July 29, 1950—After a prolonged retreat, American general Walton Walker told his troops at the Pusan Perimeter to "stand or die."

September 15, 1950—D-day at Inchon. The 1st Marine Division invaded Inchon and established a beach head at the city.

September 16-22, 1950—United States and South Korean troops broke out of the Pusan Perimeter and began an advance north.

September 26, 1950—Soldiers advancing from the Pusan Perimeter linked up with troops at the Inchon front.

September 29, 1950—Seoul was recaptured by UN forces.

October 7-8, 1950—UN troops moved north of the 38th Parallel.

October 15, 1950—President Truman met with General MacArthur on Wake Island. Since the war seemed to be nearing an end, they discussed post-war plans in Korea.

October 19, 1950—The North Korean capital of Pyongyang fell to American and South Korean forces.

October 26, 1950—American soldiers captured an enemy soldier dressed in a strange uniform. He proved to be Chinese.

November 1, 1950—The American 8th Calvary Regiment engaged in a sharp battle with Chinese soldiers near the city of Unsan in North Korea.

November 8, 1950—History's first jet against jet air battle took place near the Yalu River; during the battle an American F-80 jet shot down a Russian-built MiG-15.

November 24, 1950—MacArthur was overheard by newspaper writers who claimed he said the war would be over before Christmas.

November 26, 1950—The Chinese army launched a series of major attacks.

November 27, 1950—The 1st Marine Division was encircled at the Chosin Reservoir.

November 30, 1950—The Marines at the Chosin began a 55-mile hike in bitter cold through enemy-held territory toward the port city of Hungnam.

December 14, 1950—The great march of Marines and other troops from the Chosin Reservoir to the port of Hungnam was completed.

December 23, 1950—General Walton Walker, commander of the ground troops in Korea, was killed in a jeep accident. General Matthew Ridgway was named to take his place.

January 4, 1951—Seoul was captured by the enemy.

January 7-15, 1951—The enemy offensive was halted just south of the 38th Parallel.

January 25, 1951—General Ridgway ordered a counteroffensive.

March 14, 1951—Seoul was recaptured. This marked the fourth time in the war that the battle lines passed through Seoul.

April 11, 1951—Truman fired MacArthur.

April 17, 1951—The Chinese launched their own counteroffensive, but were stopped by UN forces.

April 19, 1951—MacArthur addressed members of Congress, who wildly cheered his words.

May 9, 1951—The U.S. Air Force, with 300 planes, struck the city of Sinuiju on the Yalu River. It was the largest raid of the war to date.

June 23, 1951—Jacob Malik, the Russian ambassador to the United Nations, urged a cease-fire and peace negotiations in Korea.

June 25, 1951—The Korean War was one year old. Combat was still fierce, but the battle lines were static with neither side making dramatic gains in territory.

July 10, 1951—Armistice talks started between the UN and the communists at the city of Kaesong, but no cease-fire agreement accompanied the discussions. Consequently the fighting continued during the negotiations.

August 23, 1951—Following bitter disagreements at the table, the peace talks were temporarily halted.

August 31 to September 3, 1951—The 1st Marine Division captured Bloody Ridge at a cost of 2,700 dead and wounded. This campaign was part of the "War of the Hills," which took place during the peace talks. During the "War of the Hills," both sides tried to take key high grounds with the intentions of improving their positions at the peace table.

September 13 to October 15, 1951—The American 2nd Infantry Division took Heartbreak Ridge while suffering 3,700 casualties.

October 25, 1951—Peace talks were resumed; they were moved to the city of Panmunjom.

February 22, 1952—The North Koreans accused the United States of dropping germ warfare bombs over North Korea. The United States denied the charges.

April 20, 1952—The UN announced that more than 50,000 communist POWs would refuse to return to communist countries if they were set free.

May 7 to May 11, 1952—Riots broke out in the Koje Island POW camp in South Korea between pro- and anti-communist prisoners.

May 12, 1952—General Mark Clark replaced General Matthew Ridgway as UN commander in Korea. Ridgway was transferred to Europe. General Mark Clark assumed command of UN ground forces.

June 23, 1952—The U.S. Air Force bombed power plants in North Korea along the Yalu River.

June 25, 1952—The Korean War was now two years old.

August 29, 1952—The Air Force bombed Pyongyang. It was the biggest air raid of the war, and many North Korean civilians were killed.

October 24, 1952—Dwight Eisenhower, running for president as a Republican, announced that if elected he would, "go to Korea."

November 4, 1952—Eisenhower was elected president with a huge majority of votes.

December 5 to December 8, 1952—President-elect Eisenhower visited Korea.

January 20, 1953—Eisenhower took the oath of office and replaced Truman as president.

March 5, 1953—Premier Joseph Stalin of the Soviet Union died in Moscow.

April 20, 1953—Operation Little Switch, an exchange of wounded and sick POWs, started in Korea. Little Switch marked the first breakthrough agreement between the UN and the communist negotiators.

June 18, 1953—South Korean president Syngman Rhee, angered over the preliminary peace agreements, released 25,000 anti-communist POWs without consulting UN commanders.

June 25, 1953—The war entered its third year.

July 13, 1953—The communists launched a major attack against positions held by South Korean soldiers.

July 27, 1953—The Korea armistice was signed at Panmunjom. A cease-fire went into effect. The war ended.

Notes by Chapter

Chapter 1
1. Clay Blair, *The Forgotten War: America in Korea 1950-1953* (New York: Anchor Press, 1989), pp. 59-60.

Chapter 2
1. Donald Knox, *The Korean War: Pusan to Chosin (An Oral History)* (New York: Harcourt Brace Jovanovich, 1985), p. 16.

2. Ibid., p. 31.

Chapter 3
1. Clay Blair, *The Forgotten War* (New York: Doubleday, 1987), p. 98.

2. Donald Knox, *The Korean War: Pusan to Chosin (An Oral History)* (New York: Harcourt Brace Jovanovich, 1985), p. 168.

3. Henry Berry, *Hey, Mac, Where Ya Been? (Living Memories of the U.S. Marines in the Korean War)* (New York: St. Martin's Press, 1988), p. 23.

4. Douglas MacArthur, *Reminiscences* (New York: McGraw-Hill, 1964), p. 349.

5. Knox, *The Korean War: Pusan to Chosin*, p. 288.

6. Ibid., p. 277.

Chapter 4
1. Donald Knox, *The Korean War: Pusan to Chosin (An Oral History)* (New York: Harcourt Brace Jovanovich, 1985), p. 459.

2. Ibid., p. 490.

3. Henry Berry, *Hey, Mac, Where Ya Been? (Living Memories of the U.S. Marines in the Korean War)* (New York: St. Martin's Press, 1988), p. 145.

4. Matthew Ridgway, *The Korean War* (New York: Doubleday, 1967), p. 93.

5. Ibid., p. 85.

6. Ibid., p. 151.

Chapter 5

1. William Manchester, *The Glory and the Dream* (Boston: Little Brown, 1974), p. 684.

2. Ibid., p. 692.

3. Henry Berry, *Hey, Mac, Where Ya Been? (Living Memories of the U.S. Marines in the Korean War)* (New York: St. Martin's Press, 1988), p. 327.

4. Matthew Ridgway, *The Korean War* (New York: Doubleday, 1967), p. 96.

5. *Newsweek* (January 22, 1951), p. 28.

Chapter 6

1. Donald Knox, *Korean War: Uncertain Victory (The Concluding Voume of an Oral History)* (San Diego: Harcourt Brace Jovanovich, 1988), p. 294.

2. Matthew Ridgway, *The Korean War* (New York: Doubleday, 1967), p. 196.

3. Knox, *The Korean War: Uncertain Victory*, p. 243.

4. Ibid., p. 237.

5. *The New York Times* (February 9, 1951).

Further Reading

Blair, Clay. *The Forgotten War.* New York: Doubleday, 1987.[*]

Farey, Carol. *Korea: A Divided Land.* New York: Dillon, 1984.

Isserman, Maurice. *The Korean War (The America at War Series).* New York: Facts on File, 1992.

Leckie, Robert. *The War in Korea 1950–53.* New York: Random House, 1963.

McNair, Sylvia. *Enchantment of the World: Korea.* Chicago: Children's Press, 1986.

Ridgway, Matthew. *The Korean War.* New York: Doubleday, 1967.[*]

Solberg, S.E. *The Land and People of Korea.* Philadelphia and New York: J.B. Lippincott Co., 1973.

*For older readers.

Internet Sites

Examining the Korean War
http://mcel.pacificu.edu/as/students/stanley/home.html

The Korean War
http://www.korean-war.com

Korean War 50th Anniversary Homepage—Department of Defense
http://korea50.army.mil/

Korean War, June 1950–July 1953—Naval Historical Center
http://www.history.navy.mil/photos/events/kowar/kowar.htm

Korean War Project
http://www.koreanwar.org/

Korean War Veterans National Museum and Library
http://www.theforgottenvictory.org

Liberation and the Korean War
http://socrates.berkeley.edu/~korea/koreanwar.html

Maps of the Korean War—United States Military Academy Department of History
http://www.dean.usma.edu/history/dhistorymaps/Korean%20War/KoreanWarToC.htm

Remembering the Korean War—U.S. Army
http://www.army.mil/cmh-pg/online/kw-remem.htm

Think Quest Time Travel to the Korean War
http://library.thinkquest.org/28386/default.htm

Index

About the Author

Mr. Stein was born in Chicago. He was graduated from the University of Illinois with a degree in history. The study of history is still his hobby. He tries to bring the excitement of history to his work. Mr. Stein has written more than eighty books—most of them histories and biographies—for young readers. The author lives in Chicago with his wife and their daughter Janna.

In 1955, two years after the Korean War concluded, Mr. Stein enlisted in the Marines, where he served three years. At the time the Korean War was still fresh in the minds of many of Mr. Stein's fellow Marines. In barracks, the author listened to the war veterans tell stories, shared their nightmares, and learned the Korean War was one of the most brutal, as well as the least understood conflict in American history.